T0057484

Crown Imperial

(Coronation March, 1937)

WILLIAM WALTON
arr. Herbert Murrill

Allegro reale (♩ = 126)

MANUAL

Sw. *mp*
(with soft reed)

PEDAL

Sw. to Ped.

5

3

10

Gt.

This arrangement incorporates the cuts made by the composer in 1963. A shorter version can be played by starting from the main theme at bar 176, cutting back from bar 209 to bar 89, and continuing from there through to the end.

© Oxford University Press 1937, 1991, and 1996. Renewed in USA 1965.

Printed in Great Britain

OXFORD UNIVERSITY PRESS, MUSIC DEPARTMENT, GREAT CLARENDON STREET, OXFORD OX2 6DP

The Moral Rights of the Composer have been asserted. Photocopying this copyright material is ILLEGAL.

15
3
20
5
sfz
5
26
sfz
f
32
Ch. mf
(+ soft Sw.)

38
p
tr
tr
Gt. marc.
45
Ch.
cresc.
51
Gt.
f
Gt.
Gt. to Ped.
57
cresc.

63
ff
reduce Sw.
f

69
3

75
+ Full Sw.

81

87
ff
Reeds
93
fff
Reeds
Gt.
f
pochiss. rall.
pochiss. meno mosso (♩ = c.120)
101
Gt.
mf
p
Sw.
Gt. to Ped. off
109
mf

118
127
poco rall.
f
136
a tempo, poco largamente
f
Gt. + Sw.
Gt. to Ped.
145
molto marcato

153
161
rit.
Solo Reeds
169
ff
Gt.
a tempo
primo sub.
f
177

183
3

189

194
3
+ Full Sw.

200

206
ff
Reeds
211
mf
cresc.
Gt.
219
227
rit. - - - - - - - molto
Grandioso
ff
fff

236
(largamente)
molto marc.
245
254
largamente
262
tr
tr

271
a tempo primo sub.
ff (Sw. box closed)
277
3
282
288
Open
molto marc.

295
con tutta forza
Full Ped.
303
poco più largamente
312
321